Group/Guided Reading Notes

Contents

Red Planet

Lost in the Jungle

The Broken Roof

The Lost Key

The Willow Pattern Plot

Submarine Adventure

Introduction

Oxford Reading Tree stories at Stages 5 to 9 continue to feature the familiar characters from previous stages in stories that reflect the experiences of most children. The magic key, discovered at Stage 4, also takes children into exciting fantasy adventures, widening and enriching their reading experience.

The stories still use natural language, phonically decodable words and high frequency words, all illustrated with funny and engaging pictures. Reading them will enable children to practise different reading skills, and continue to develop their word recognition and language comprehension.

Using the books

This booklet provides suggestions for using the books for guided, group and independent activities. The reading activities include ideas for developing children's *word recognition* **W** and *language comprehension* **C** skills. Within word recognition, there are ideas for helping children practise their phonic skills and knowledge, as well as helping them to tackle words that are not easy to decode phonically. The language comprehension ideas include suggestions for teaching the skills of prediction, questioning, clarifying, summarising and imagining in order to help children understand the text and the whole stories. Suggestions are also provided for speaking, listening, drama and writing activities.

Reading fluency

To support children in developing fluency in their reading, give them plenty of opportunities to revisit the stories. This includes:
- rereading independently
- rereading with a partner

- rereading at home
- listening to audio versions of the story (e.g. Talking Stories)
- hearing the story read to them by others as they follow the printed text.

Rereading and rehearing helps children develop automatic word recognition and gives them models of fluent, expressive reading.

Comprehension strategies

Story	Comprehension strategies taught through these Group/Guided Reading Notes				
	Prediction	Questioning	Clarifying	Summarising	Imagining
Red Planet	✓	✓	✓	✓	
Lost in the Jungle	✓	✓	✓	✓	✓
The Broken Roof	✓	✓	✓	✓	
The Lost Key	✓	✓	✓		✓
The Willow Pattern Plot	✓	✓	✓	✓	✓
Submarine Adventure	✓	✓	✓	✓	

Vocabulary and phonic opportunities

Each story contains many decodable words, providing lots of opportunities to practice phonic and word recognition skills. The chart shows the tricky words used in each book. The tricky words are common but do not conform to the phonic rules taught up to this point – children will need support to learn and recognise them. If children struggle with one of these words you can model how to read it.

Red Planet	Tricky words	boots, broken, buggy, called, computer, float, floor, four, good, little, mountains, one, out, people, pieces, pull(ed), some, space, spaceman, spacesuit, there, want, were, what, where
Lost in the Jungle	Tricky words	air, alligators, angry, behind, birthday, broken, buildings, called, city, explorers, found, full, good, have, jungle, know, lady, love, might, mind, monkey, place, through, throw, waterfall, wonderful, years
The Broken Roof	Tricky words	asked, broken, can't, climbed, clothes, fence, field, find, first, handle, hole, home, house, know, mangle, mother, new, one, picture, push(ed), roof, school, secret, some, table, tea, through, two, want, washing, who, worked, workmen
The Lost Key	Tricky words	boy, broken, buy, called, can't, fault, flew, found, mower, next, painted, pictures, rain, remind, round, rubbed, started, threw, tied, trainers, two, would, wouldn't
The Willow Pattern Plot	Tricky words	bought, called, caught, cruel, friends, gasped, heard, loved, oh, ready, something, sound, waited
Submarine Adventure	Tricky words	aeroplane, amazing, engines, excited, huge, looked, muddled, oh, phew, properly, right, wrong, young

Curriculum coverage chart

	Speaking, listening, drama	Reading	Writing
Red Planet			
PNS Literacy Framework (Y2)	2.3, 3.2, 4.1, 4.3	**W** 5.3 **C** 7.1	9.5, 12.3
National Curriculum	Working towards Level 2		
Scotland (5–14)	Level A	Level A	Level A
N. Ireland (P3/Y3)	1, 2, 4, 6, 7, 8, 9, 11	1, 3, 5, 8, 11, 12, 14, 15, 16, 17	1, 2, 5, 8, 10, 11, 12
Wales (Key Stage 1)	Range: 1, 2, 3, 5 Skills: 1, 2, 3	Range: 1, 2, 4, 5, 6 Skills: 1, 2	Range: 1, 2, 4, 7 Skills: 1, 2, 3, 4, 5, 6
Lost in the Jungle			
PNS Literacy Framework (Y2)	2.1, 2.3, 3.2, 4.1	**W** 5.2 **C** 7.1	9.3, 10.1, 11.2
National Curriculum	Working towards Level 2		
Scotland (5–14)	Level A	Level A	Level A
N. Ireland (P3/Y3)	1, 3, 6, 8, 10, 11, 14	1, 3, 5, 8, 11, 12, 14, 15, 16, 17	1, 2, 3, 5, 8, 10, 11, 12, 13
Wales (Key Stage 1)	Range: 1, 3, 5, 6 Skills: 1, 2, 3	Range: 1, 2, 3, 4, 5 Skills: 1, 2, 3	Range: 1, 2, 3, 5, 6 Skills: 1, 2, 3, 4, 7, 8

Key

C = Language comprehension   Y = Year

W = Word recognition   P = Primary

In the designations such as 5.2, the first number represents the strand and the second number the bullet point

Curriculum coverage chart

	Speaking, listening, drama	Reading	Writing
The Broken Roof			
PNS Literacy Framework (Y2)	1.1, 2.1, 3.1, 3.2, 4.1	W 5.4 C 8.2	10.1, 11.3
National Curriculum	Working towards Level 2		
Scotland (5–14)	Level A	LevWel A	Level A
N. Ireland (P3/Y3)	1, 5, 6, 11	1, 3, 5, 8, 11, 12, 13, 14, 15, 16, 17	1, 2, 3, 5, 8, 10, 11, 12, 13
Wales (Key Stage 1)	Range: 1, 2, 3, 5 Skills: 1, 2, 3, 4, 5, 6	Range: 1, 2, 3, 4, 5 Skills: 1, 2	Range: 1, 2, 3, 5, 7 Skills: 1, 2, 3, 7, 8
The Lost Key			
PNS Literacy Framework (Y2)	1.3, 2.1, 3.3, 4.1	W 5.2 C 8.2	9.1, 9.5, 10.2
National Curriculum	Working towards Level 2		
Scotland (5–14)	Level A	Level A	Level A
N. Ireland (P3/Y3)	1, 2, 4, 5, 6, 7, 8, 10	1, 3, 8, 11, 12, 14, 15, 16, 17	1, 2, 3, 5, 10, 11, 12, 13
Wales (Key Stage 1)	Range: 1, 2, 3, 4, 5 Skills: 1, 2, 3	Range: 1, 2, 4, 5, 6 Skills: 1, 2	Range: 1, 2, 3, 4, 5, 7 Skills: 1, 4, 7

Curriculum coverage chart

	Speaking, listening, drama	Reading	Writing
The Willow Pattern Plot			
PNS Literacy Framework (Y2)	Y2 2.3, 4.1, 4.2	Y2 **W** 5.1, 5.2, 5.3 **C** 6.1, 7.1, 8.3	Y2 9.1, 11.2
National Curriculum	Working towards level 2		
Scotland (5–14)	Level A	Level A	Level A
N. Ireland (P3/Y3)	1, 2, 5, 6, 8, 10, 11	1, 3, 6, 11, 12, 14, 15, 16, 17	1, 2, 3, 4, 5, 10, 11, 12, 13
Wales (Key Stage 1)	Range: 1, 2, 5, 6 Skills: 1, 2, 3, 5, 6	Range: 2, 4, 5, 6 Skills: 1, 2, 4	Range: 1, 2, 3, 7 Skills: 1, 2, 3, 4
Submarine Adventure			
PNS Literacy Framework (Y2)	3.1, 4.1	Y2 **W** 5.2, 5.5 **C** 7.4, 8.3	9.2
National Curriculum	Working towards level 2		
Scotland (5–14)	Level A	Level A	Level A
N. Ireland (P3/Y3)	1, 2, 5, 6, 8, 10, 11	1, 3, 6, 11, 12, 14, 15, 16, 17	1, 2, 3, 5, 7, 10, 11, 12, 13
Wales (Key Stage 1)	Range: 3 Skills: 2, 3, 4, 5, 6	Range: 2, 5, 6 Skills: 1, 2	Range: 1, 3, 6, 7 Skills: 1, 2, 3, 5, 7

Red Planet

> **C** = Language comprehension **R, AF** = QCA reading assessment focus
> **W** = Word recognition **W, AF** = QCA writing assessment focus

Group or guided reading

Introducing the book

C *(Prediction)* Turn to the back cover and hide the title. Ask: *What do you think the children are looking at? Where do you think they might be*?

C *(Clarifying)* Look at the front cover and read the title together. Have the children predicted the setting correctly?

● Look briefly through the story at the illustrations and talk about what is happening.

Strategy check

Remind the children to keep place with a finger at the beginning or end of a line.

Independent reading

● Ask children to read the story. Praise and encourage them while they read, and prompt as necessary.

W Ask the children to show you the spoken words in the story and point out the speech marks.

Assessment Check that children:

● *(R, AF1)* recognise the smaller words in the compound words 'spacemen' and 'spacesuit'

● *(R, AF2)* identify where speech marks are used to show dialogue.

Returning to the text

C *(Summarising)* Ask: *What did the children discover on the Red Planet?*

C *(Imagining)* Find 'open' on page 8. Ask: *What is the opposite of 'open'? How would the story have been different if the door had been closed?*

C *(Questioning)* Turn to page 17 and ask: *Do you think Chip is right to be nervous about going outside? What dangers might there be out there?*

C *(Prediction)* Turn to page 28 and ask: *What would have happened if the spacesuits had gone 'pop'?*

W Ask the children to find more compound words in the story and make a list (page 5 'inside', page 10 'nobody', page 16 'outside'). Check that they can recognise the smaller words.

W Look at 'filled' on page 27 and read it. Ask the children to write the word with just one 'l'. Ask: *How would you read this word now? What has changed?* Point out how the vowel phoneme changes from a short vowel sound to a long one.

Group and independent reading activities

Objective Draw together ideas and information from across a whole text (7.1).

C *(Summarising)* Discuss the main settings in the story with the children.

- Ask them to close their eyes and picture the settings in their mind. Encourage them to share their images with a partner.

- Write the settings on the board and talk about the order of them, e.g. the beginning: the garden; the middle: the rocket and the Red Planet; the end: the rocket and the garden. Show how the order of events is circular:

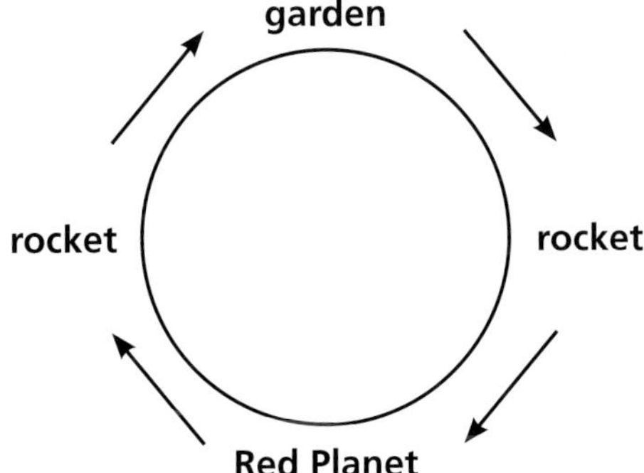

- Working in pairs, ask the children to write down the settings and what the children in the story do and see in each. Ask: *In which setting did the most things happen? Why do you think this is?*

Assessment **(R, AF2)** Are the children able to locate evidence in the text to support their ideas?

Objective Select from different presentational features to suit particular writing purposes (9.5).

C *(Imagining)* Prepare six pieces of paper cut in the shape of speech bubbles for each child.

- Ask the children to focus on the illustrations of Floppy on pages 3, 10, 15, 18, 20 and 28.

- Ask them to read the parts that say what Floppy is thinking and to write what they think he would say in the speech bubbles.

Assessment **(R, AF2)** Do the children leave out the speech marks when writing in speech bubbles. Are they able to retrieve information from the text?

Objective Know how to tackle unfamiliar words that are not completely decodable (5.3).

W Write the characters' names on the board: 'Wilf', 'Chip', 'Floppy' and 'Nadim'.

- Say the names with the children and clap and count the syllables.

- Ask the children to look through the story and collect words with more than two syllables in them ('pretended', 'computer', 'adventure', etc.).

Assessment **(R, AF1)** Do the children understand that the number of letters in the word is not the same as the number of syllables?

Speaking, listening and drama activities

Objective Respond to presentations by commenting constructively (2.3). Work effectively in groups (3.2). Adopt appropriate roles in small or large groups and consider alternative courses of action (4.1).

- Ask the children to suggest other things that might have happened on the Red Planet, e.g. the space creatures showed the children the way out, or the children took the space creatures home with them.

- In groups the children take the roles of Wilf, Chip, Nadim, Floppy and the space creatures.

- Suggest they choose a different story line and work together to create a short play describing what happens.

- Ask some groups to act out their play to the others.

- Ask the audience for constructive comments on the plays. Also encourage the audience to ask the actors questions which they must answer in role.

Objective Consider how mood and atmosphere are created (4.3).

- Refer back to the activity on story settings (garden, rocket, planet).

- Working in groups, ask the children to think about the type of music/ sounds that would create the right mood and atmosphere in each setting, e.g. garden: birds singing; rocket: computer noises and bleeps; planet: whistling (wind) and sounds to create tension.

- If possible give each group some musical instruments to recreate the sounds they have discussed.

Writing activities

Objective Wordprocess short non-narrative texts (12.3).

- Ask the children to imagine that the characters, including Floppy, need to have a passport to travel into space.

- Set up a template passport using a wordprocessing program. Model how to write the character profile, drawing information from the story, e.g.

PASSPORT

Name:	Wilf
Girl/Boy:	boy
Age:	7
Hair:	brown
Home:	Earth
Character:	likes computers, brave, has good ideas

- Ask the children to choose a character, note down information about that character and enter the information onto the template.

- Print off so children can draw a picture of his or her character in the box.

Assessment *(R, AF2)* Are children able to retrieve information from the text? *(W, AF3)* Have the children presented the text effectively?

Lost in the Jungle

C = Language comprehension   **W, AF** = QCA writing assessment focus

W = Word recognition   **R, AF** = QCA reading assessment focus

Group or guided reading

Introducing the book

C *(Clarifying)* Look at and discuss the cover with the children. Ask them to read the title and the blurb on the back cover.

C *(Prediction)* Encourage the children to say what they think the setting of the story will be.

C *(Clarifying)* Look briefly through the story at the illustrations to confirm the children's ideas.

Strategy check

Remind the children to break longer words into parts to make them easier to read.

Independent reading

● Ask children to read the story. Praise and encourage them while they read, and prompt as necessary.

C *(Questioning)* As you listen to children, ask them questions about the story, e.g. on page 13, ask: *How do you think the children are feeling?*

W Find the word 'branch' on page 10. Check how the children work out how to read this word and praise them for sounding out and blending the sounds. Repeat for 'alligators' on page 12 and 'explorers' on page 15.

Assessment Check that children:

● *(R, AF1)* read high frequency words on sight

● *(R, AF2)* read with expression appropriate to the punctuation.

Returning to the text

C *(Clarifying)* Turn to page 32, and ask: *Who is Biff referring to when she says 'I know where we can get a monkey too'?*

(C) *(Clarifying)* Ask: *Which setting is the more frightening, the jungle or the Lost City? Why?*

(C) *(Imagining)* The author doesn't give the explorers' names. Ask: *What names would you give the explorers?*

(C) *(Clarifying)* Ask the children to think of several reasons why Biff, Kipper, Chip and Anneena liked the explorers and why they were prepared to help them.

(C) *(Imagining)* Look at page 28. Ask: *How do you think the children felt?* Find the words on page 29 that describe the Lost City and how amazing it is.

(C) *(Clarifying)* Talk about the different settings in the story. Ask: *Which setting makes a better place to have an adventure?*

(W) Read page 9. Point out the statement, 'That monkey looks cross.' *Ask: Why doesn't Kipper say 'That monkey looked cross'?* Discuss how one is in the present and one is in the past.

Group and independent reading activities

Objective Draw together ideas and information from across a whole text (7.1).

(C) *(Summarising)* Ask the children to close their eyes and picture the different settings in the story ('home', 'jungle', 'Lost City'). Encourage them to add detail and then share their images with a partner.

- Discuss the settings as a group.

- Ask the children to write a sentence describing each setting under the headings: 'home', 'jungle' and 'Lost City'.

- Then ask them to look through the book to find two things found only in each setting/illustration.

- Talk about how the settings in the story influence what the characters do and feel, e.g. in the jungle the children are amazed by what they see around them.

Assessment *(R, AF2)* Are the children able to locate evidence in the text to support their ideas?

Objective Compose sentences using tense consistently (present and past) (11.2).

- Write the following sentences on the board or on sentence strips:

  Biff gives Mum a plant.
  Anneena comes to play.
  The magic takes them to a jungle.
  The children see a monkey.
  They run through the jungle.
  They fall into a big net.

- Discuss the verbs and their tenses in the sentences.

- Ask the children to rewrite the sentences as if they were telling a story about something that has already happened.

Assessment *(R, AF6)* Are the children able to write the irregular past tense verbs 'came', 'took', 'saw', 'ran' and 'fell'?

Objective Spell with increasing accuracy and confidence, drawing on word recognition and knowledge of word structure (5.2).

(W) Discuss how the word 'birthday' on page 1 can be split into two smaller words.

- Ask the children to look through the text and collect other examples of compound words: 'greenhouse', 'waterfall', 'nobody', 'everything'.

- Can they think of any other words that are made up of two smaller words?

Assessment *(R, AF1)* Are the children able to find words within other words?

Speaking, listening and drama activities

Objective Listen to others in class (2.1). Respond to presentations by commenting constructively (2.3). Work effectively in groups (3.2).

- Talk about what sort of people the explorers are. Encourage the children to each contribute one idea.

- Ask the children to work with a partner and think about how they would describe the explorers in the story. Encourage them to use a dictionary, thesaurus or computer software to find appropriate words and phrases.

- Ask the children to share their ideas and decide which description is the most effective.

 Respond to presentations by commenting constructively (2.3). Adopt appropriate roles in small groups (4.1).

- Ask the children to work in small groups. Give each group one of the following scenes from the story to act out:

  Walking out into the jungle
  Seeing the snake
  Stepping out onto the bridge
  Going through the waterfall
  Climbing the steps
  Seeing the Lost City

- Encourage the children to use the appropriate expressions to accurately convey the feelings of the characters.

- Ask groups to present their scene to the rest of the children.

- Praise children who make constructive comments on the performances afterwards.

Writing activities

Objective Maintain consistency in non-narrative, including purpose and tense (9.3). Use planning to establish clear sections for writing (10.1).

- Look closely together at the illustrations of the jungle in the story.
- Ask the children to suggest words that describe the features of the jungle. Draw up a list of words and phrases.
- Explain to the children that they are going to write a short piece for a travel brochure describing the jungle and what visitors will find there.
- Encourage the children to plan their writing first, e.g.

  Introduction – How to get there
  What it looks like
  What animals can be found
  What there is to do (river trips; Lost City; hunting; animal watching)
  Accommodation (tent)

- Children write and illustrate their article.

Assessment *(R, AF2)* Are children able to retrieve information from the text?

(W, AF3) Have the children presented the text effectively?

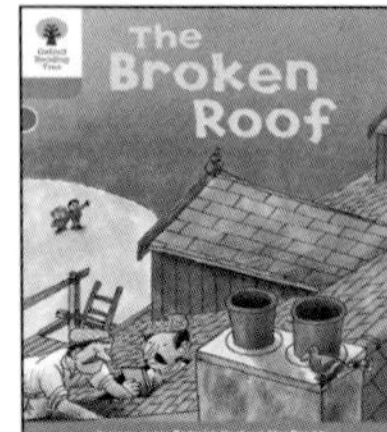

The Broken Roof

> **C** = Language comprehension **R, AF** = QCA reading assessment focus
>
> **W** = Word recognition **W, AF** = QCA writing assessment focus

Group or guided reading

Introducing the book

C *(Prediction)* Look at the front cover together. Encourage the children to say what they think the setting of the story will be. Ask: *Is it in the present day or in the past?*

C *(Clarifying)* Look briefly through the story at the illustrations to confirm the children's ideas.

Strategy check

Remind the children to notice speech marks and read accordingly.

Independent reading

- Ask children to read the story. Praise and encourage them while they read, and prompt as necessary.
- Encourage them to read to the end of the sentences and then return to words which cause them difficulty.

C *(Questioning)* As you listen to children, ask them questions about the story, e.g. on page 8 ask: *How does Kipper feel about the house being taken to school? What is he worried about?*

W Find the word 'display' on page 9. Check the children can read the syllables in the word (dis–play).

W Help children to read the new names on page 17 by sounding out the phonemes in each syllable.

Assessment Check that children:

- *(R, AF1)* use a range of strategies to work out new words such as 'mangle'
- *(R, AF2)* read with expression appropriate to the grammar and punctuation

- *(R, AF3)* understand that this magic adventure takes the characters back in time.

Returning to the text

C *(Questioning)* On pages 30–31, ask: *How do you think the roof of the little house was mended? What would Mum have thought?*

C *(Clarifying)* On page 30, ask: *Why do you think Chip is not smiling?*

C *(Clarifying)* Look at pages 16–17. Ask: *Why did each group of children think that the others were funny?*

C *(Summarising)* Ask: *What kind of person was the cook? Was she kind? Was she bossy? Do you think the children liked her? How do we find out about her?*

W Ask the children to find one long word in the book. Ask them to break the word up into syllables. *What were the other children's names? How many syllables are in each name?*

W Find the words 'washing' on page 6 and 'kitchen' page 20. Praise children for sounding out and blending the phonemes to help them read the word.

Group and independent reading activities

Objective Engage with books through exploring interpretations (8.2).

C *(Summarising)* Ask the children to choose one of the characters from the story and to write a short description of them without stating the character's name.

- Instruct the children to swap their descriptions with a partner, read the descriptions and guess the name of the character.

Assessment *(W, AF6)* Do the children read their own descriptions to check for sense before swapping?

Objective Speak with clarity and use appropriate intonation when reading and reciting texts (1.1). Use question marks (11.3).

C *(Clarifying)* Working in pairs, the children take turns to choose a page from the story and read a line of speech, using the appropriate expression. He or she then asks: 'Who said this?'

- The partner then guesses the character, finds the spoken words in the text and points to the punctuation that shows where the speech starts and ends.

- Pairs then write some questions that Biff, Chip and Kipper might want to ask Victoria, Edward and Will. Remind them to end each question with a question mark.

Assessment *(R, AF3 AF4)* Do the children read speech with expression and recognise speech marks?

Objective Read and spell less common alternative graphemes (5.4).

- Ask children to find words in the text that end in 'le' ('mangle' and 'handle' page 4, 'little' page 7).

- Can they think of any other words that end in 'le'? (bundle, candle, ladle, jungle).

- Ask: *What other words that rhyme with these words end with 'el'?* (tunnel, funnel, gravel, etc.).

- Encourage children to draw up a list of '-le' words and '-el' words.

Speaking, listening and drama activities

Objective Listen to others in class (2.1). Ensure that everyone contributes (3.1). Work effectively in groups (3.2).

- In pairs, ask the children to collaborate to draw up a list of features they can see in and outside the Victorian house, using the illustrations from pages 14–28.

- Ask the children to share their findings with the rest of the group and to talk about the advantages and disadvantages of living in the old house. Encourage them to discuss the things they would miss, e.g. television, cars.

Objective Speak with clarity (1.1). Adopt appropriate roles in small groups (4.1).

- Ask the children to work in groups of four. Explain that you would like them to divide up into pairs.

- Ask them to turn to pages 16–17 and to reread the text and look at the picture.

- One pair then introduces themselves to the other pair in the same way that the children introduce themselves in the book. Encourage them to say a few lines about themselves as well, e.g. 'I am seven years old, I have brown hair, I have one brother and one sister.'

- Make sure the children speak in a clear voice.

Writing activities

Objective Maintain consistency in non-narrative, including purpose and tense (9.3). Use planning to establish clear sections for writing (10.1).

- Discuss the illustration on pages 20–21. Talk about the objects found in the kitchen and write their names on the board, e.g. 'mangle', 'range', 'scullery', 'gas lamp', 'flat iron'.

- Ask the children to draw a picture of each of the items and then underneath write a short description of how they work.

- Encourage them to use this information to write a guide to a Victorian kitchen, describing the things that can be found there and how the kitchen items work.

- Some children may like to describe how the Victorian kitchen is different to the modern-day kitchen. Ask: *Which do you think is better?*

Assessment *(R, AF2)* Are children able to retrieve information from the text? *(W, AF3)* Have the children presented the text effectively?

The Lost Key

> **C** = Language comprehension   **R, AF** = QCA reading assessment focus
>
> **W** = Word recognition   **W, AF** = QCA writing assessment focus

Group or guided reading

Introducing the book

- **C** *(Prediction)* Hide the title and look at the cover with the children. Ask them to say what they think is happening.

- Read the title and ask the children to read the blurb on the back cover.

- **C** *(Clarifying)* Look briefly through the story at the illustrations. Ask the children to think about the lost key. Can they think of a reason why there are so many characters in the story?

Strategy check

Remind the children to take note of punctuation and to read with appropriate expression.

Independent reading

- Ask children to read the story. Praise and encourage them while they read, and prompt as necessary. Encourage reading with expression, pausing at commas.

- **C** *(Questioning, Clarifying)* On page 2, ask: *What did Mum say? Who can read it with expression?*

- **C** *(Prediction)* After each stage of the story, ask: *What might happen next?*

Assessment   Check that children:

- *(R, AF1)* read high frequency words with confidence

- *(R, AF1)* use a range of strategies to work out new words

- *(R, AF3)* know how to read the direct speech with different intonation from the rest of the sentence.

Returning to the text

C *(Clarifying)* Ask: *Did Mum know why the key was important to the children? Which pages tell us what Mum feels about the key?* (pages 5 and 23).

C *(Clarifying)* On page 10, ask: *Why has the man got a bump on his head?*

C *(Clarifying)* On page 13, ask: *Why has the man got a different mower?*

W On page 3, ask the children to find the word 'rocket'. Ask them to find another word on the same page which rhymes with 'rocket'.

W On page 8, ask the children to find two words which sound the same but which are spelt differently ('two' and 'to'). Ask the children to give you examples of different sentences in which the two versions are used.

W On page 11, find 'could'. Discuss the phoneme sound and which letter is silent. Can the children think of any other words that have this spelling pattern? ('would'). Ask: *What other words have the same phoneme sound?* ('wood', 'good').

W *(Questioning)* Discuss the actions of the boys after they broke the greenhouse glass on page 11. Ask: *What would you have done? What would have been the right thing to do?*

Group and independent reading activities

Objective Explain ideas using imaginative and adventurous vocabulary (1.3). Engage with books through exploring and enacting interpretations (8.2).

C *(Imagining)* Ask the children to suggest other places where Kipper might have lost the key, e.g. the swimming pool, at school, in the shops.

- Choose one of the suggestions and make up a few opening lines, e.g. 'Kipper forgot he had the key in the pocket of his swimming trunks when he went swimming. When he got dressed again, he looked in his pocket, but the key was not there…'

- Ask the children, in pairs, to decide what happens next, who finds the key and how Kipper gets it back again.

- Invite some of the children to share their ideas with the rest of the group.

Assessment *(W, AF3)* Do the children use the structure of the story to think of new events and outcomes.

Objective Select from different presentational features to suit particular writing purposes on paper (9.5).

C *(Prediction)* **You will need** three pieces of paper cut in the shape of speech bubbles for each child.

- Ask the children to look at the illustrations of Mum on page 25, Wilf on page 26 and Kipper on page 27. Explain that they are going to write speech bubbles to show what each character might be saying.
- Remind them to write the name of the character on the back of the pieces of paper.

Assessment *(W, AF6)* Do the children write speech using the correct syntax and without speech marks?

Objective Spell with increasing accuracy and confidence, drawing on word recognition and knowledge of word structure (5.2).

W Write the following words on the board: 'lock', 'agree', 'appear', 'tie', 'obey', and 'happy'.

- Ask the children: *Was Kipper lucky or unlucky to lose the key? Did Mum like or dislike having to pay for the key?*
- Ask the children to write the negative form of the words on the board, by adding either 'un-' or 'dis-' to the beginning of each.
- Ask them to put the words into sentences.

Assessment *(R, AF6)* Do the children reread their words to check that they sound correct?

Speaking, listening and drama activities

Objective Listen to others in class, ask relevant questions (2.1). Listen to each other's views and preferences (3.3). Adopt appropriate roles in small or large groups and consider alternative courses of action (4.1).

- Together look at the picture of Kipper on page 27.

- Invite children to take the role of Kipper and, in turn, sit in the 'hot seat'. Ask children to describe an adventure they think Kipper would like to have.

- Encourage the 'audience' to ask 'Kipper' questions about the adventures.

- Decide as a group which adventure they think sounds the most exciting.

Writing activities

Objective Draw on knowledge and experience of texts in deciding and planning what and how to write (9.1). Use appropriate language to make sections hang together (10.2).

- Write the following sentences on the board:

  What did you lose?

  How did you lose it?

  What happened to it?

  Did you find it?

  How did you find it?

  Was it damaged?

- Talk about some of the items that you or the children have lost, using the questions on the board as prompts.

- Ask the children to write their own story about losing something, using the prompts to help them structure their writing.

- Remind them of time language: 'first', 'then', 'next', 'after', 'in the end' to make sections of their writing hang together.

Assessment *(W, AF3)* Have children sequenced the events in their story correctly?

The Willow Pattern Plot

C = Language comprehension   **R, AF** = QCA reading assessment focus

W = Word recognition   **W, AF** = QCA writing assessment focus

Group or guided reading

Introducing the book

- Discuss the cover and read the title with the children. Establish any knowledge the children may already have about willow pattern pottery.

- **C** *(Prediction)* Ask the children to read the back cover blurb and ask them to say what they think will happen in the story.

- Look briefly through the book to confirm the children's ideas. Use some of the decodable and tricky words as you discuss some of the pictures (see chart on page 4).

Strategy check

Remind the children to try various strategies to work out new or unfamiliar words.

Independent reading

- Ask the children to read the story. Praise and encourage them while they read, and prompt as necessary.

- **C** *(Clarifying)* Ask occasional questions about the story to make sure the children understand what is happening: *Why are the people in the story dressed differently from Biff, Chip and Nadim? Why did the guards trip over on the bridge?*

- **C** *(Summarising)* Ask children to retell the story in just four or five sentences.

Assessment Check that children:

- *(R, AF1)* use phonic knowledge to sound out and blend the phonemes in words, particularly the tricky words

- read with appropriate expression, pausing at commas, and changing tone for exclamations and questions.

Returning to the text

C *(Questioning, Clarifying)* Ask the children: *Why was Kim Shee unhappy? Why couldn't she marry Chang, the man she loved? Why do you think her father wanted her to marry a rich man?*

C *(Summarising, Prediction)* Ask children to describe the land where Chang and Kim live. Ask: *Which country do you think this story is set in*? (China).

W On page 11 point to the word 'cruel' and help children to sound it out. Point out how 'uel' makes one sound.

C *(Imagining)* Look at pages 8–9. Ask the children to imagine living in a world that was just one colour. Ask: *Would you like it? Which colour would you choose? What colours would you miss?*

Group and independent reading activities

Objective Read independently and with increasing fluency longer and less familiar texts (5.1). Know how to tackle unfamiliar words that are not completely decodable (5.3).

W Ask children to read pages 1–3 alone.

- Ask them to copy down any words they find difficult. Pool the words and ask volunteers to suggest strategies for working them out.

- Ask children to spell the word without looking at it. Repeat for the next few pages of the story.

Assessment *(R, AF1)* Do the children suggest a range of strategies for working out the words?

Objective Spell with increasing accuracy and confidence, drawing on word recognition and knowledge of word structure, and spelling patterns (5.2).

You will need to write the following words on the board: 'like', 'kind', 'do', 'appear', 'tidy'.

W Talk about how the prefixes 'un- 'and 'dis- 'can change words to mean the opposite.

- Write the word 'happy' on the board and ask the children to find the opposite meaning in the text (page 10).

- Look at the words on the board and ask the children to add the correct prefix to give them the opposite meaning.
- Ask the children to use a word bank or dictionary to add other similar words to the list.

Assessment *(R, AF1)* Do the children reread the word to check it sounds right?

Objective Read and spell less common alternative graphemes including trigraphs (6.1).

- **W** Turn to page 19 and ask the children to find the word 'garden'.
- Ask them which two letters make the sound 'ar'.
- Ask them to find another two words on the same page in which three letters make the same sound ('uar' in 'guards' and 'ten' in 'listen').
- Ask the children to look at page 20 and find a word where four letters make one sound' ('augh' in 'caught').

Assessment *(R, AF1)* Are the children able to work out the sounds in the word 'afraid'?

Objective Draw together ideas and information from across a whole text (7.1).

- **C** *(Summarising)* Ask the children to turn to pages 8 and 9, read the description of the garden and look at the illustration.
- Ask them to tell you the key features of the landscape.
- Write the children's suggestions on the board, e.g. 'bridge', 'house', 'lake', 'lemon trees'.
- Encourage the children to tell you what happened at each place.
- Some children could attempt to draw a map of the garden, writing labels and captions to show the events of the story.

Assessment *(R, AF2)* Do the children use the text to retrieve information?

Objective Explain their reactions to texts, commenting on important aspects (8.3).

- **C** *(Clarifying, Imagining)* Ask the children to reread the story from page 10, focusing on the sentences that describe Kim Shee's father.
- Invite children to tell you what sort of person Kim Shee's father is. Record their descriptions on the board.
- Ask: *How do you think he felt after his daughter had run away? What advice would you give him?*

- Ask: *Would the story have been the same if he had let Kim Shee see Chang?*

Assessment *(R, AF3)* Do the children refer to the text and illustrations for details?

Speaking, listening and drama activities

Objective Respond to presentations…commenting constructively (2.3). Adopt appropriate roles in small or large groups and consider alternative courses of action (4.1). Present part of traditional stories and their own stories for members of their own class (4.2).

- Ask the children to work with a partner. Tell them to take the roles of Kim and Chang and to read the dialogue from pages 13–16 as if it were a play.

- Next, ask them to make up their own dialogue, but this time to imagine that Chang has his own plan on how he and Kim can get away from the garden. Ask: *What route of escape has he planned?* (e.g. under the bridge). *What items will he bring to help them?* (e.g. a boat).

- Ask some of the children to perform their new dialogue to the rest of the class or group. Encourage the 'audience' to comment constructively on the group's performance.

Writing activities

Objective Draw on knowledge and experience of texts in deciding and planning what and how to write (9.1). Compose sentences using tense consistently (11.2).

- If possible, show some willow pattern plates to the children.

- Read Nadim's words on the last page to the children.

- Ask them to suggest other stories for the willow pattern plate. Model how to write some of their suggestions as opening sentences in the past tense.

- Ask the children to write their own willow pattern stories and illustrate them in blue and white for a class display.

Assessment *(W, AF3)* Is the story well-organised and carefully illustrated?

Submarine Adventure

> **C** = Language comprehension   **R, AF** = QCA reading assessment focus
>
> **W** = Word recognition   **W, AF** = QCA writing assessment focus

Group or guided reading

Introducing the book

C *(Prediction)* Look at the cover and ask the children: *Where are the characters? Look at the children's faces. Are they enjoying this adventure? How do you know?*

- Ask the children to read the back cover blurb.

Strategy check

Remind the children to sound out words to work them out, and to reread sentences to check the context.

Independent reading

- Ask the children to read the story. Praise and encourage them while they read, and prompt as necessary.

W Encourage the children to use their knowledge of sounds and syllables to work out new words, e.g. 'explores'.

W Check that the children split the compound words, e.g. 'birthday', 'headlights', into their component parts.

C *(Clarifying)* Check that the children realise the words Professor Tangle mishears rhyme with the last words in the sentences spoken by the children.

C *(Summarising)* Ask the children to retell the story in four or five sentences, encouraging them to use high and medium frequency words.

Assessment Check that children:

- *(R, AF1)* read the high and medium frequency words on sight
- *(R, AF2)* understand what a fuse is on page 23
- *(R, AF3)* use comprehension skills to work out what is happening in the story.

Returning to the text

C *(Questioning, Clarifying)* Ask children: *Why does the Professor ask the children to go onboard? Why does the Professor think that the children came in a plane?* Ask the children to explain why the Professor gets muddled. Ask: *Do you think the children knew they were going to get out of the cave just in time?*

C *(Imagining)* Ask the children to describe how it might feel to go down into the sea in a submarine. Ask: *Would it be dark or light in the deep sea? Would it be cold or warm?*

C *(Summarising)* Ask the children to retell the end of the story in one sentence.

Group and independent reading activities

Objective Spell with increasing accuracy and confidence, drawing on, for example, knowledge of word structure and spelling patterns, including common inflections (5.2).

W Write the word 'submarine' on the board. Discuss with the children that someone who works in a submarine is called a 'submariner'.

- Ask the children to name some professions or job titles they know that have the same ending. Write the word 'sailor' on the board. Talk to the children about the use of the vowels 'o' and 'e' as a suffix for job titles.

- Ask the children to think of different professions or jobs and use a word bank or dictionary to find job titles with '-er' and '-or' endings.

Assessment *(R, AF1)* Do the children recognise the same sound has different spellings?

Objective Spell with increasing accuracy and confidence, drawing on, for example, knowledge of word structure and spelling patterns, including common inflections (5.2). Read high and medium frequency words independently and automatically (5.5).

W Ask the children to work in pairs and reread each page where the Professor mishears one of the children.

- Ask them to write down what the child said and what the Professor thought he or she said.

- For each, ask: *Can you think of another phrase with a rhyming word that the Professor could have thought he heard?* For example, on page 12 'You ate some stew…' instead of 'You flew…'

- Explain that they can make up nonsense words that rhyme if they cannot think of another alternative.

- Ask them to write down their ideas, then read them out to another pair of children.

Assessment *(R, AF1)* Can the children read the high and medium frequency words without prompting? Can they think of words with the same sounds?

Objective Explain their reactions to texts, commenting on important aspects (8.3).

C *(Summarising)* Discuss the main setting of this story (the sea) with the children, and ask them to say which other stories they have read that have the same or similar settings.

- Ask the children to look through *Mirror Island* and to list the similarities and differences between the story settings in that book and *Submarine Adventure.*

- Ask: *Are the characters similar?* (children meet elderly man). *Is the story line similar?* (find treasure but don't take it).

- Ask: *Which setting did you prefer and why? Which is the most exciting setting and why?*

Assessment *(R, AF7)* Do the children know other sea/treasure themed stories?

Objective Use syntax and context to build their store of vocabulary when reading for meaning (7.4).

C *(Clarifying)* Ask the children in pairs to look through the book and find words that are to do with submarines and piloting them, e.g. 'diving machine', 'crew', 'hatch', 'engines', 'dive', 'button', 'lever', 'handle', 'switch', 'fuse', 'tool box'.

- Record the children's suggestions on the board.

- Invite children to read out a word and then tell you its definition.

- Ask the children to draw an outline of a submarine and write the context words inside. Can they think of other words to do with submarines?

Speaking, listening and drama activities

Objective Ensure that everyone contributes, allocate tasks, and consider alternatives and reach agreement (3.1). Adopt appropriate roles in small or large groups and consider alternative courses of action (4.1).

- Ask the children to sit close together in groups of three and imagine they are sitting inside a submarine.

- Ask the children to contribute a thought each about what they can see and hear, and how they feel.

- Next, ask them to imagine that something exciting happens, e.g. they see a shark, or go into a cave. Ask them to say how they feel now.

Writing activities

Objective Sustain form in narrative, including use of person and time (9.2).

- Ask the children to look through the illustrations in the story and focus on those from inside the submarine: pages 12, 13, 16 and 17, 24 and 25, 26, 27, 30, 31.

- Discuss how the children must have felt when they discovered the lights of the submarine didn't work (pages 22–27) and then when Professor Tangle fixed them by putting in a new fuse (page 28).

- Tell the children to close their eyes and imagine they are sitting in the submarine.

- Ask them to write a description of what they see in front of them.

- Children share their writing with the rest of the group.

Assessment *(W, AF1)* Do the children write imaginatively? *(W, AF6)* Do the children use punctuation correctly in their sentences?

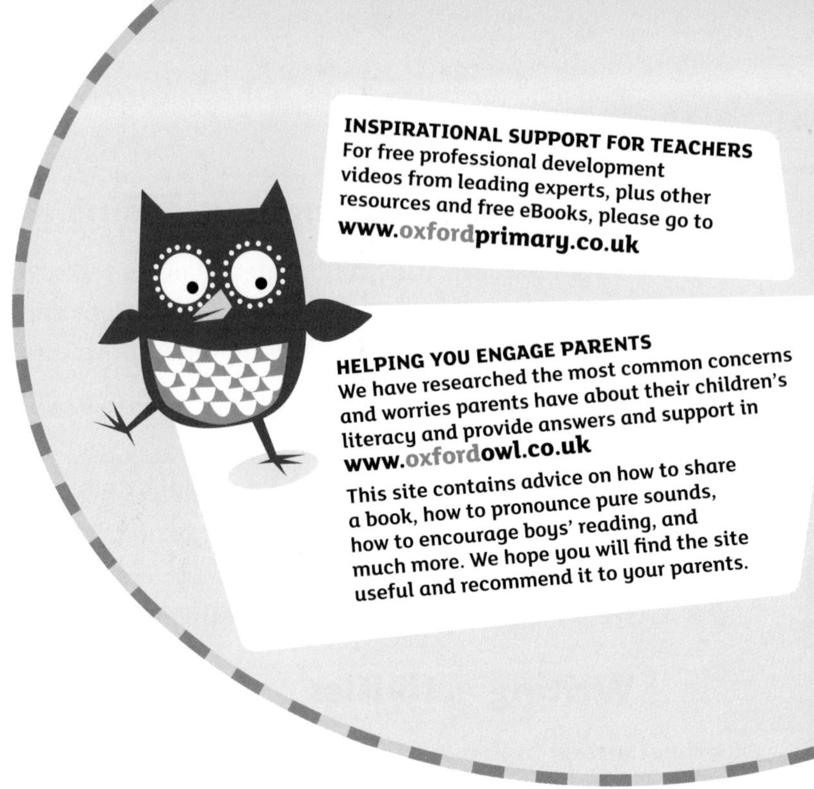

OXFORD
UNIVERSITY PRESS

Great Clarendon Street, Oxford OX2 6DP

Oxford University Press is a department of the University of Oxford. It furthers the University's objective of excellence in research, scholarship, and education by publishing worldwide in

Oxford   New York
Auckland Cape Town Dar es Salaam Hong Kong Karachi
Kuala Lumpur Madrid Melbourne Mexico City Nairobi
New Delhi Shanghai Taipei Toronto

With offices in

Argentina Austria Brazil Chile Czech Republic France
Greece Guatemala Hungary Italy Japan Poland
Portugal Singapore South Korea Switzerland
Thailand Turkey Ukraine Vietnam

Oxford is a registered trade mark of Oxford University Press in the UK and in certain other countries

Text © Oxford University Press 2008

Written by Lucy Tritton and Liz Miles, based on the orginal characters created by Roderick Hunt and Alex Brychta.

The moral rights of the author have been asserted

Database right Oxford University Press (maker)

First published 2008
This edition published 2011

All rights reserved. No part of this publication may be reproduced, stored in a retrieval system, or transmitted, in any form or by any means, without the prior permission in writing of Oxford University Press, or as expressly permitted by law, or under terms agreed with the appropriate reprographics rights organization. Enquiries concerning reproduction outside the scope of the above should be sent to the Rights Department, Oxford University Press, at the address above

You must not circulate this book in any other binding or cover and you must impose this same condition on any acquirer

British Library Cataloguing in Publication Data

Data available

Cover illustrations Alex Brychta

ISBN: 978-0-19-848312-0

10 9 8 7 6 5 4

Page make-up by Thomson Digital

Printed in China by Imago

Paper used in the production of this book is a natural, recyclable product made from wood grown in sustainable forests. The manufacturing process conforms to the environmental regulations of the country of origin.